Walks

TAMAR AND TAVY COUNTRY

Denis McCallum

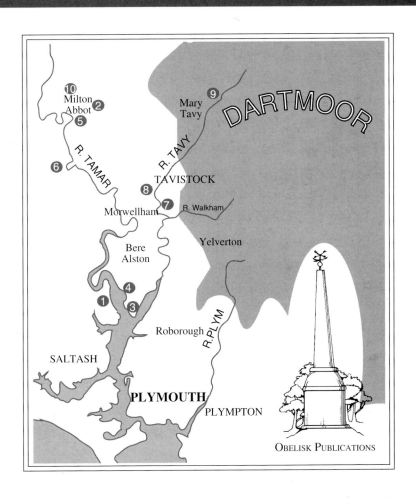

OBELISK PUBLICATIONS

OTHER 'WALKING' TITLES FROM OBELISK PUBLICATIONS INCLUDE:
Walks in the Shadow of Dartmoor, Denis McCallum
Walks in the South Hams, Brian Carter
Diary of a Dartmoor Walker, Chips Barber
Diary of a Devonshire Walker, Chips Barber
Ten Family Walks on Dartmoor, Sally & Chips Barber
Ten Family Walks in East Devon, Sally & Chips Barber
The Great Walks of Dartmoor, Terry Bound
Rambling in the Plymouth Countryside, D. Woolley & M. Lister
Walking "with a Tired Terrier" In and Around Torbay, Brian Carter
The Templer Way, Derek Beavis

For further details of any of our titles, please contact us at the address below or
telephone Exeter (0392) 68556

PLATE ACKNOWLEDGEMENTS
All sketch maps by Sally Barber based on drawings by the author
Cover photographs by Chips Barber

*This book is dedicated to the memory of Hedley Rawling, who first aroused
my interest in the topography and history of Devon and Cornwall.*

*First published in 1992 by
Obelisk Publications, 2 Church Hill, Pinhoe, Exeter, Devon
Designed by Sally Barber
Typeset by Sally Barber
Printed in Great Britain by*

CONTENTS

INTRODUCTION

The River Tamar rises a mere five miles or so from the north Cornish coast, and marks the boundary between Devon and Cornwall. The Tavy is much shorter, rising on northern Dartmoor and joining the Tamar just upstream of the city of Plymouth. Both run through highly mineralised areas – in the nineteenth century their valleys were the scene of intense mining activity. These rivers, especially the Tamar, were also a vital part of the transport system of those days. A flourishing barge traffic developed, and a river port and canal were constructed to serve the area, it being far easier and cheaper to carry goods by water than to haul them up and down steep hills by horse and cart or packhorse. The mining machinery of those days was also largely driven by water power, and some of the leats constructed to take water to the mines are still in existence, while others can still be traced.

The wonderful scenery of the area, along with its mining remains and the quays and lime kilns associated with river transport, make the exploration of Tamar and Tavy country uniquely rewarding. This is necessarily a "where to go" book, so I have only been able to touch on the rich historical background – the industrial archaeology of this area would fill twenty books of this size – but I hope you will find these snippets of interest.

Personally I dislike carrying a back-pack, so you will find that all but two of these ten walks pass a pub or snack bar where you can have lunch if you wish. At the start of each I try to give you some idea of the terrain you will encounter, how muddy, rough and steep it is, and of the distance involved (generally between 5 and 7 miles). I have also tried to grade them into easy, moderate, or strenuous, but I'm taking a big risk here as this is such a subjective matter: so much depends on age and fitness, also on weather conditions and the state of the paths and bridleways. I'm sure the most strenuous of these walks would seem easy to a fit man of 20, and what might be easy in dry summer weather could well be a slog in heavy rain with ankle-deep mud underfoot! So if you disagree with my assessments – I can only apologise in advance. Except after prolonged dry spells, stout boots are recommended for all these walks, whilst in soggy winter weather wellies are virtually essential.

Unfortunately it is not possible to avoid a certain amount of road walking, but I have tried to keep it to a minimum and to restrict it to fairly quiet lanes. Even so, on a couple of the walks it is necessary to take to fairly busy highways for short distances. I can only urge you to take the greatest care here.

On footpaths and bridleways always stick to the route as described (you will be trespassing if you deviate), remember to shut all gates (unless obviously left open for a purpose), keep dogs under control and take your litter home with you. Here endeth the lesson.

The information in this book is correct to the best of my knowledge at the time of writing, but bear in mind that things never stand still: footpaths get diverted or extinguished, pubs close or stop doing food, waymarks and footpath signs appear and disappear. Always take an OS map with you, the large-scale 1:50 000 at least, to supplement the sketch maps in this book.

Easy. Muddy in places after heavy rain, **very** muddy if you go along the shore! 5¼ or 5½ miles. OS 1:50 000 Map 201, 1:25 000 Map 1349.

This is a delightful little walk along footpaths and quiet roads through countryside which is comparatively unfrequented in spite of its proximity to Saltash and Plymouth. Most of it is within sight and sound of the tidal river Tamar, and optionally along its shoreline.

Turn off the A38 on to the A388 road for Callington at the Carkeel roundabout near the Tamar Bridge. In about one and a half miles you will pass the Holland Inn. A quarter of a mile further on, in Hatt, take the right-hand turning signposted Botus Fleming. On reaching the crossroads in this hamlet (half a mile), take the left-hand turning signposted Landulph and Cargreen. Caution: this road is narrow, winding, and very steep as you descend to a T-junction in about one mile. Turn right here on to another narrow road which brings you to a crossroads known as Landulph Cross in one mile. Turn right here and you come to Landulph church at the bottom of the hill in three-quarters of a mile, where you should find room to park.

From here your route leads back up the hill you have just driven down, but you might like to make a short diversion down to the shore. If so, turn left past the church and walk to the entrance to Landulph House. Climb over the stile by the gate on the right into a rough marshy field to follow the path alongside the grounds of Landulph House. On your right is a wide expanse of marshland (known with great originality as "The Marsh") protected from the river by a high dyke. At the edge of this marsh there is a holy well; in the nineteenth century attempts were made to promote this as a spa. However, the river flooded the area and scuppered this little scheme to put Landulph on the map.

The path leads through a gate and down on to the beach. You are now at the mouth of Kingsmill Lake, a creek of the Tamar leading up to Moditonham and Coll007gett Quays, once busy with the river barge traffic carrying lime and farm produce but now in peaceful ruin. Downriver are the twin Tamar bridges, Brunel's pioneering railway bridge completed in 1859, and the modern road bridge, continuously a-twinkle with traffic, which was built over a hundred years later. Opposite are the mouths of Tamerton Creek and the river Tavy, each with its railway bridge carrying what used to be the main Southern Region line to Waterloo, but is now the single-track Tamar Valley line to Bere Alston and Gunnislake. The vessels moored in the river downstream are ammunition barges belonging to the Royal Navy Armament Depot at Bull Point.

The OS map indicates a footpath following the shore to Cargreen, but although I have walked it I don't recommend it. It is a very muddy route and involves some scrambling over slippery, weedy rocks: you will not be too popular in the

Spaniards Inn at Cargreen if you arrive plastered with stinking river mud! Also, it is very easy to get cut off by the tide here: you can only get around the two rocky promontories a few hundred yards along the beach for an hour or so either side of low water, and thereafter you have no choice but to continue following the indentations of the shoreline to Cargreen, as your retreat will be cut off. Timing is absolutely crucial. However, if you do decide to risk the shoreline route you

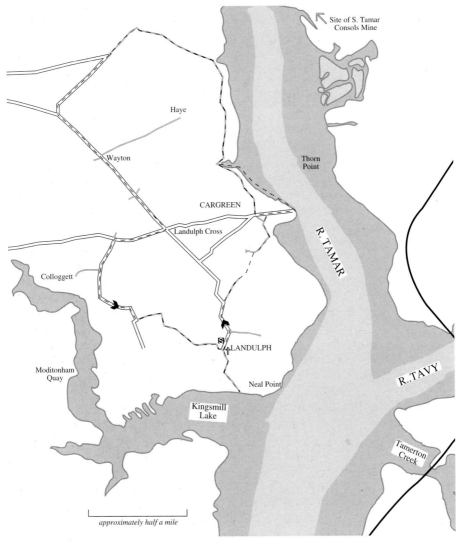

leave it at the recreation ground at Cargreen, where there is a spring just below the embankment to wash the worst of the mud off your boots.

The best way to Cargreen, though, is to retrace your steps to the church and continue up the hill until you come to a footpath sign on your right in a quarter of a mile. This path leads uphill between hedges for a short distance, then you have to negotiate a gate into an open field. Follow the left-hand hedge downhill and climb a stile into the next field. Although no obvious path can be discerned from here, if you walk straight down across the middle of the field towards the opposite hedge you will find a hidden stile leading into a delightful sunken lane which will take you down into the village. Follow the road past the recreation ground – where it starts to climb notice an old well on the left. Branch right along a lane which leads to the lower part of the main street. Turn right here, then follow it down towards the river. The Spaniards Inn, which commands fine views across the Tamar, is the last building you come to on the left. You can sample their bar snacks and selection of real ales if you time it right and get there at lunchtime: it only takes about half an hour to walk there from Landulph by the footpath, and about an hour if you go along the shore.

From here the path leads through the car park below the pub and down a short flight of steps to the beach. This is passable at most states of the tide, but like the shoreline path to Cargreen from Landulph it is very muddy. You **can** walk along the rocks above the beach, but these are slippery and treacherous (my wife and I recently ended up in a tangled heap here – fortunately no bones were broken, but they could have been). It is better to proceed up the main street of Cargreen and take the first turning on the right: this road (Coombe Drive leading to Coombe Lane) meets the footpath in a quarter of a mile.

If you **do** walk along the beach you will be looking across the river to Thorn Point on the Bere Alston – Bere Ferrers peninsula between the Tamar and the Tavy. If you are a bird-watcher, this stretch may take you some time, especially at low tide in winter, as many species of ducks and waders can be observed here: besides the usual curlews, redshanks, turnstones and sandpipers, you may see bar-tailed and black-tailed godwits and avocets, and there's always the chance of spotting the odd rarity. The duck family is typically represented by mallard, widgeon, shelduck and tufted duck, and you also sometimes get teal, pochard and shoveler. Besides these you will always see cormorants and flocks of common and black-headed gulls.

The shore path and Coombe Lane meet at the head of a small creek, where boats are laid up in the winter. Follow the road through three gates: from this stretch look across the river at an area of marsh, and just to the left of this you will see what appear to be mounds of sand scattered down the hillside with an ivy-grown chimney to one side. This is all that remains of South Tamar Consuls silver/lead mine, the workings of which extended out under the river. These were flooded when the river broke in one day in the middle of the last century, but as the mine was providentially closed at the time, no one was drowned.

In half a mile you will come to a couple of houses by a small creek (Salter Mill). A footpath is signposted on your left here, but it only leads up to Haye Farm, through the farmyard and back to the head of the little creek on Coombe Lane. Although the farm lane leads up to the St. Mellion–Landulph road at Wayton, this is not a public right of way, so we will carry on along the road: climb the hill and take the first turning on the left at a place called Tinnel, and you will come to the St. Mellion–Landulph road near North Wayton. Turn left here. This is still a relatively quiet road, but is the busiest you will encounter on this walk. It brings you back to Landulph Cross in one mile. Turn right here, then left in quarter of a mile down a lane marked with a "No Through Road" sign. Continue down this road, which commands fine views over Kingsmill Lake to Botus Fleming, once famous for its cherry orchards, for about half a mile until you come to a "Public Bridleway" sign on the left pointing to a track between hedges. Take this, and after a short ascent follow it steadily downhill towards Landulph. Eventually you pass between the garden of Lower Marsh Farm and "The Marsh", and enter the hamlet via the farm road, which comes out beside the church where you started the walk.

If you take the shortest route this walk is five and a quarter miles, but if you take the longer route along the shore to Cargreen it is about five and a half miles: only an extra quarter of a mile, but it feels a lot more!

WALK TWO

MILTON ABBOT – CHILLATON

Moderate. Can be muddy in places after rain, and very muddy in one spot. 6¾ miles. OS 1:50 000 Map 201, OS 1:25 000 Maps 1327 (SX 48/58) and 1340.

The first part of this walk is not too exciting as it is mainly along roads, albeit quiet ones. However, the after-lunch part is much more interesting.

Take the B3362 (Tavistock–Launceston) road to Milton Abbot. Turn off beside the church and park by the roadside at the bottom of the churchyard.

Walk eastwards along the main road and turn left up a lane with a "No Through Road" sign opposite the Village Hall. In a few yards you will see a Public Bridleway sign pointing up a track to the left. Go up here and through the gate into a field. There is no obvious path, but head straight up the field to the right-hand gateway. Bear slightly right across the next field to the gate at the top right-hand corner and go through it.

Follow the right-hand hedge up the next field to the gate into the road.

Turn right and walk along the road for almost quarter of a mile to a road junction. Turn left up the hill and carry on until you descend to another road junction in three-quarters of a mile. Bear left here (Ramsdown Cross). In a quarter of a mile a minor road turns off to the right. Take this and follow it for three-quarters of a mile, mostly downhill. Just beyond a very long low new house, before you come to Chillaton House, turn off right along an unsurfaced track leading steeply down towards the village of Chillaton. This emerges on to the Chillaton–Lifton road – if you turn right here you will soon come to the Chichester Arms in the centre of the village, where bar snacks may be obtained.

After lunch, retrace your steps along the Lifton road by which you entered the village and follow it for a mile to a farm called Warracott. Just beyond here turn off left up an unsurfaced drive signposted Public Bridleway. This swings left in about 200 yards – a sign indicates a footpath striking off to the right across a field. Ignore this and carry on up the drive. In about a quarter of a mile you come to a farm called

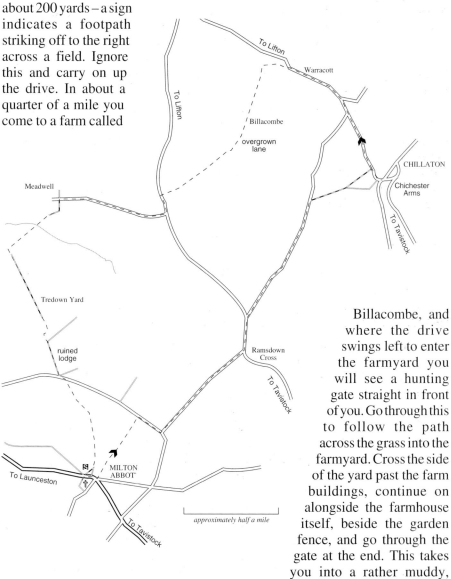

To Lifton

Warracott

To Lifton

Billacombe

overgrown lane

CHILLATON

Meadwell

Chichester Arms

To Tavistock

Tredown Yard

ruined lodge

Ramsdown Cross

To Tavistock

To Launceston

MILTON ABBOT

To Tavistock

approximately half a mile

Billacombe, and where the drive swings left to enter the farmyard you will see a hunting gate straight in front of you. Go through this to follow the path across the grass into the farmyard. Cross the side of the yard past the farm buildings, continue on alongside the farmhouse itself, beside the garden fence, and go through the gate at the end. This takes you into a rather muddy, overgrown lane leading uphill to a metal gate. Go through this and continue up across the field, following the prominent ruts in the surface, until you reach the corner of a hedge. Follow along beside this hedge through two more gates, and in the last field you pass the tower of a wind-powered pump. All the way across the fields you have wonderful views across to Dartmoor, with the Elizabethan Sydenham House and the prominent churches of Marystow and Coryton on opposite sides of the Lyd valley in the foreground. Just past the wind-pump tower, a gate brings you out on to a road. Turn left here, then right in 200 yards, and carry on along this road down to Meadwell.

Where the road bears to the right in this hamlet, you will see in front of you a building with a postbox in the wall – in the entry to the left here you will see a Public Footpath sign. Note the old well here. Follow the indication of the footpath sign into a narrow lane which emerges through a hunting gate into a field. You need to bear pretty sharply left here, not diagonally across the field as the yellow arrow on the gate seems to indicate. Enter the next field and proceed diagonally to the right down towards the stream where it passes through a strip of woodland. Here the stream runs under a culvert, and as farm vehicles converge on the crossing it is usually extremely muddy.

Bear diagonally left up across the next field, making for the left-hand end of a strip of woodland. Soon you will see a gate, which leads into an unsurfaced lane. Turn left here. If you look back from this stretch you will see the Georgian Kelly House, the towers of Kelly and Bradstone churches and the town of Launceston on its hilltop on the other side of the Tamar valley in the distance.

The lane will take you past the yard of Tredown farm and past the turning down to the farmhouse. Just before you emerge on to the road you pass the ruins of Kelly Lodge near what is left of the old estate gateway.

On reaching the road, from where you can look down on your starting point, Milton Abbot, turn left – a few yards along you will see a Public Footpath sign on the right. Climb the stile here into the field and continue along beside the hedge into another field. There are often sheep in most of the fields you will be crossing, so keep dogs under control. In fact, unless they are small enough to pick up and carry, I wouldn't think dogs would be able to negotiate the stiles on this stretch: it would be better to continue along the road back to Milton Abbot.

Just before you get to the end of the second field you will see a stile on the right. This is a two-stage affair: a stile over the hedge and another over the sheep-wire inside it. Negotiate these, which bring you into the corner of a field: bear diagonally left across it. You will see another stile to the right of the gate in the opposite corner. This one is a three-stage stile: a wooden one over the sheep-wire, two projecting stepping stones and an old brass-topped curtain rail in the hedgetop to hold on to, stepping stones and another wooden stile on the other side.

The field you have now entered is a long narrow one; you need to bear left diagonally across it. If unsure of the direction, head for Milton Abbot church tower. Do not go through the gateway you will see on your right, but keep going until another one comes into view at the bottom left of the field. Go through this one, then immediately left through an opening into another long narrow field. Carry on down beside the right-hand hedge to the stile in the wooden fence at the bottom. This brings you into a short lane leading down to the main road through Milton Abbot, which it joins right opposite the church. In this lane a couple of streams emerge through the wall, one gushing through a stone trough: these are very useful for washing the mud off your wellies before getting into the car.

WALK THREE
BERE FERRERS – BERE ALSTON

The next two walks are "railway walks" – they assume that you reach the Bere Alston peninsular between the Tamar and the Tavy by means of the Tamar Valley Line from Plymouth, so are based on the two railway stations in the area, but of course you can go by car if you prefer.

As mentioned in Walk One, the single track Tamar Valley Line was once the main Southern Region line to Waterloo via Exeter and Salisbury, looping round the western and northern flanks of Dartmoor. It now goes no further than Bere Alston, with a spur to Calstock and Gunnislake just over the Cornish border, although at present there is some talk of re-opening the line as far as Tavistock to relieve congestion on the road to Plymouth. At the time of writing, the most convenient train to catch for these walks leaves Plymouth North Road station at 9.30 am. Parking is available here for a fee. You can also catch it at St. Budeaux Victoria Road at 9.41 am, and near this halt is a free car park. The trains run roughly every 2–2½ hours, but precise timings can be ascertained from BR leaflets available at local stations. BR also issue leaflets on the Tamar valley line describing points of interest along the route, walks and bus services from the various stations in the summer months and the dates of guided walks from the railway led by the local Countryside Ranger in July, August and September.

The first walk entails leaving the train at Bere Ferrers. Don't forget you have to notify the guard when he collects your fare that you wish to alight here. It is a moderate walk, but although it involves an ascent from virtually sea level to 490 feet it somehow doesn't feel that much of a climb because it is so gradual. The first part is through woods which can be muddy after rain, the second part is mainly along quiet roads. 6½ miles. OS 1:50 000 Map 201, OS 1:25 000 Map 1349.

From Bere Ferrers station, turn right down the road into the village and right again at the T-junction at the bottom. Go down this road past the Post Office and a pub called the Plough and you come to the Tavy estuary. The road bears around to the left along the shore, and in a short distance swings sharply around to the left before heading inland. Don't follow it, but carry on along the lane that runs straight on along the shoreline. On some high spring tides this lane can be flooded for a short while, in which case you would either have to wait for the tide to ebb or take the inland road, which finishes up at the same place, anyway.

From this stretch you can look across the estuary to the mouth of Blaxton Creek with the remains of its quay and limekiln. The point on the other side of this creek has a crenellated lookout where I spent many hours watching birds as a teenager. Like the Tamar estuary, this is an excellent place for ornithologising.

The shore lane bears left through a gate into a footpath in a hundred yards or so, runs through a narrow belt of trees and bushes on the edge of the low cliff above the estuary, and eventually goes through another gate into a field where there are often sheep. It then runs along between the bottom of a garden and the shore, emerging above a bit of saltmarsh at Gnatham creek, which it reaches by crossing the bottom of someone's lawn, so don't go above the "private" sign erected here. Follow the path through the saltmarsh to the road.

Beside the bungalow you will see to your left a few yards along this road a

Public Footpath sign points into the woods. Follow this through a gate, and you find yourself on a track which follows a stream up a wooded valley. The woods are coniferous at first but more mixed higher up. Follow this track up the valley for a

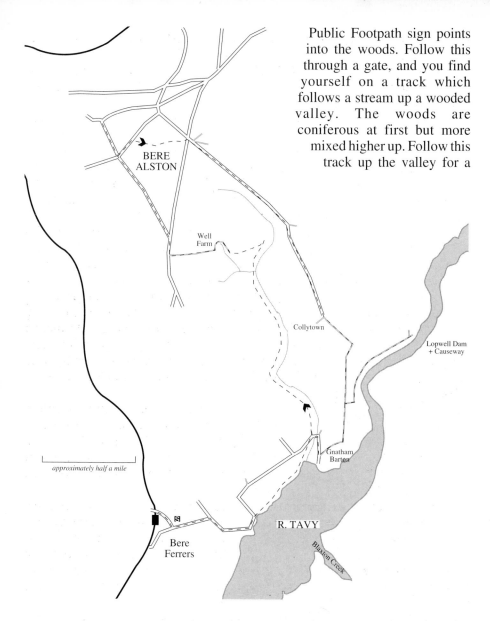

BERE ALSTON

Well Farm

Collytown

Lopwell Dam + Causeway

Gnatham Barton

approximately half a mile

Bere Ferrers

R. TAVY

Blaxton Creek

mile, keeping close to the stream: don't be tempted to take any of the much more well-defined forestry tracks leading uphill as these simply take you back the way you have come, but higher up the hill. The last of these in particular seems to insist on you taking it, but nevertheless ignore it and keep right along the lower path nearest the stream, even though it looks pretty tenuous compared to the other one.

Eventually you will see a clearing on your left where a field cuts into the woodland, the path then starts to climb out of the valley. When you encounter another path coming up from the other direction, turn sharp left to follow it uphill: it brings you to a stile into a field. There is no obvious path here, but bear left across the field and follow the left-hand hedge. This will take you to a gate leading to a track between a hedge on your right and some lawns and gardens on your left. This brings you to a gate into the yard of Well Farm. Turn left and go up through the farm buildings – the track brings you to the Bere Alston–Bere Ferrers road. Turn right, and in a few yards you come to a fork: bear left here, and you come to a crossroads on the outskirts of Bere Alston in half a mile. Carry straight on down the main street and you reach a pub called the Edgcumbe on the right, where you can obtain liquid refreshment at least. Unfortunately this pub recently stopped serving food, but a few yards further on down Station Road there is a snack bar and takeaway where you can get lunch.

After lunch, retrace your steps back up the main street to the crossroads, but this time turn left here. In a couple of hundred yards a Public Footpath sign points across the Recreation Ground. Cross the rugby and soccer pitches diagonally to the right-hand corner of the field (this walk is best avoided on Saturday afternoons!), where the path goes over a stile and along the edge of the next field, emerging on to the road at a junction. Take the road opposite the footpath stile, signposted "Collytown". Walk straight on down this road. In one and a quarter miles it starts to descend steeply into the Tavy valley. You get good views across the river to Maristow House and park and down the estuary to its junction with the Tamar, where it is spanned by the viaduct over which you would have passed earlier if you travelled by train.

About halfway down this hill you will come to a track turning off on your left: this leads up the valley through the woods to Lopwell dam, where water is abstracted to supply Plymouth. At low tide it is possible to walk across a causeway to the other bank. If you have time to spare, it makes a pleasant extension to the walk. There are various remains of the old Lopwell silver-lead mine scattered throughout these woods.

In about one and three-quarter miles from the start of this road you come to a hairpin bend to the right with a road going straight on. Follow the road around the bend to the right (the road going straight on just goes to Gnatham Farm) – you reach the head of Gnatham creek again and the bottom of the track up through the woods you followed before lunch. Now it is just a matter of retracing your steps to Bere Ferrers station, either by the shore path or along the road if you want a change.

The walk takes roughly two hours to Bere Alston and two hours back, so you should catch the 3.00 p.m. train at Bere Ferrers comfortably if you don't linger in the Edgecumbe too long! Don't take these train times as gospel, by the way – always check them before setting out, as they can change.

Don't forget to give a hand signal for the train driver to stop and pick you up.

If you wish you can do this walk in reverse, starting at Bere Alston and lunching at the Plough in Bere Ferrers.

FIGURE-OF-EIGHT WALK IN BERE ALSTON AREA

This second "railway walk" starts from Bere Alston station, and here you don't have to request the train crew to stop – they have to anyway. It is a fairly strenuous walk, involving a lot of climbing, some very muddy and boggy areas to cross and three streams to wade – wellies required at any time of year. 6¾ miles. OS 1:50 000 Map 201, OS 1:25 000 Map 1349.

I have classified this walk as "fairly strenuous" because it entails two separate descents into the Tamar valley from Bere Alston and therefore two ascents of 425 feet, the second one entailing a climb of 160 feet in a mere tenth of a mile (1 in 3.3, or 30%). The first part of the walk takes you on a tour of the wooded valleys to the north of Bere Alston between the town and the Tamar, while the second part takes you down to the Tamar again, but this time to the west.

Turn right under the two bridges when you leave the station yard. The first bridge carries the line from Plymouth, the second the line to Gunnislake. When it was a main line station, you used to change trains here for the Calstock and Gunnislake branch line. Now trains go no further north: instead the driver changes ends and the train simply "reverses" on to what used to be the Gunnislake branch line.

A few yards down the road you will see a stile on your left with a footpath sign and a notice that "this footpath has been adopted by Bere Alston Youth Club". Climb the stile and descend the field steeply down the valley to a stile at the edge of the woodland. From here the path descends the wooded valley above the stream. Where it divides, take the right-hand path heading downhill towards the Tamar valley, past the remains of the old Tamar Valley silver/lead mine. Eventually the path runs alongside the stream, and crosses it to the right via a ford and stepping stones just before it plunges into the Tamar at Butts Pill (ignore the path branching off to the left continuing downstream above the river). The stepping stones are usually awash, so wellies are advisable, unless you take off your boots or shoes and wade. Before doing this it is worth carrying on to the bottom of the path where it ends above the Tamar – by looking downstream you will see the town of Calstock on the Cornish bank with its graceful viaduct carrying the railway across the river. Such grace was achieved by the builders in the face of numerous difficulties, both physical and financial. It was built to join what was originally the East Cornwall mineral line from Kelly Bray and Callington to the main line at Bere Alston.

The path runs along above the Tamar for about 200 yards before passing in front of some cottages: in fact it passes between the cottages and their front gardens, in one of which a topiary representation of a bird may be seen. These cottages are idyllically situated, being right on the river and a good three-quarters of a mile from the nearest tarmac road.

Bear right away from the river up the valley just after the cottages. Where the path divides into two, take the right-hand branch continuing up the valley on the right bank of the stream: the other branch crosses the stream by some railway sleepers, and a notice here forbids entry into University of Plymouth property: by the way it is divided into numbered sections and staked out in plots I would imagine that it is run as an ecological study area by the Department of Environmental Science.

A long but steady climb up the valley and across another stream brings you to an access road to several houses, which in turn brings you out on to the road at Tuckermarsh by one of the bridges over the disused and overgrown section of the old main line to Waterloo.

Turn right and carry on climbing up this very quiet road. You pass a house on the left called "Wheal Jenny" after a forgotten mine which is reputed to have operated in this area ("Wheal" being the Cornish word for mine). From a gateway on the right a little further on you get a very good view of the Tamar valley from Calstock up towards the old river port of Morwellham. Immediately below you can be seen the chimneys and dumps of Gawton copper and arsenic mine on the banks of the Tamar, as well as an old lime kiln at Gawton quay. Many years ago a local friend showed me a "blue pool" on the site of Gawton mine, copper salts being responsible for the colour. It is difficult to realise, surveying today's peaceful scene, that for much of the last century this whole area resembled the Rhondda valley in its heyday, though perhaps not so black: everywhere were mine shafts and adits, with chimneys belching out arsenic fumes, blighting the vegetation. Now there are only ruins, but miles of levels and caverns still extend beneath your feet, and even beneath the rivers Tamar and Tavy.

Carry on until you come to a crossroads on the outskirts of Bere Alston. Go straight across and on down Drakes Park. Turn left at the bottom, passing the Parish Hall and the Social Club on your right – in a few yards you come to the snack bar on your right (where you can lunch) and the Edgcumbe pub a little further on.

After lunch, retrace your steps back along Station Road for a third of a mile until you come to the fork just after the garage on the left. Turn left here down a road signposted "Braunder" and "Helstone". In a quarter of a mile it crosses a bridge over the line from Plymouth to Bere Alston – on the other side of this bridge is a signpost pointing left to Braunder. Take this road (ignore the footpath sign on the left for the moment), which leads past Collins Farm down to Braunder Farm. Here the lane appears to end at a gateway into a cattle pen, but in fact it continues through this and out of the gateway on the other side of the pen. If you are unhappy about going through this when it is full of cattle, ask at the farmhouse. If it isn't feasible to get through here, go back to the footpath sign at the top of the lane by the railway bridge. This path takes you over a stile and into the yard of Collins Farm. Pass along the edge of this into the next narrow field, then through a gap into a much larger field. Follow the left-hand hedge beside the railway embankment nearly to the bottom of this, then bear right down to a stile beside a house. After this stile a short path brings you into the lane down to Lockeridge Farm, which is near the site of an old silver/lead mine of the same name. Turn right down this, go through a gate and on down to the farm. When you reach the farmyard in half a mile, turn left through the yard down to the stream, ignore the path leading steeply up to the left, and follow the path to the right down the valley. This path

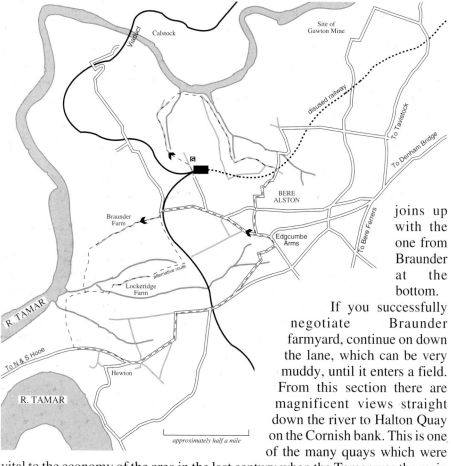

joins up with the one from Braunder at the bottom.

If you successfully negotiate Braunder farmyard, continue on down the lane, which can be very muddy, until it enters a field. From this section there are magnificent views straight down the river to Halton Quay on the Cornish bank. This is one of the many quays which were vital to the economy of the area in the last century when the Tamar was the main artery for the barge traffic carrying coal, lime, manure, agricultural produce and mineral ores. Beyond Halton Quay can be seen Pentillie Castle amongst its woods on the hilltop.

The path continues down across this field along an unfenced track and enters another field, where it is no longer so well-defined. Turn left here along the hedge at the top of the field, heading for the gap in the corner. From this gap you will see a stile in the hedge at the bottom of the next triangular field. Make for this, and climb over it. You then descend a rough flight of steps leading down to a wooden bridge over the stream in the valley bottom, which joins the Tamar a few hundred yards further down.

Cross the bridge and squelch across the very marshy valley bottom to the other side. Here you join the path running down the valley from Lockeridge Farm, your alternative route. Turn right and follow the path down towards the river until it strikes off left up a sort of gully into a field. Bear left at the top of the gully and in a few yards you will see a short lane leading steeply down into the next valley between what remains of hedges. It is a bit tangled at the bottom of this, but a yellow arrow directs you to bear to the left here, and across another marshy bit you should see a small plank bridge over the stream. Cross this, and ahead is a stile leading to a very steep ascent to another stile: this bit is like the side of a cliff – an alpenstock would be handy. Carry on climbing to a third stile: the worst is now over, and it might be a good idea to sit on this one to recover and enjoy another wonderful view, this time up river to Cotehele Quay. Cotehele House, once one of the seats of the Edgcumbe family but now owned by the National Trust, is just beyond. On the top of the hill above Cotehele may be seen a curious folly in the shape of a three-sided "church tower", from which warning signals are reputed to have been exchanged with Maker church tower by the staffs of Cotehele and Mount Edgcumbe Houses, indicating that the Edgcumbes were en route between the two!

The climb across the next field is much gentler. Go through the gate at the top into the road which leads up from North and South Hooe. There were once silver/lead mines here also, extending under the Tamar, and it is said that the beat of the paddle wheels of the steamers plying the river could be heard in the upper levels of these mines. Turn left, and continue along this gently-climbing road for a mile to a bridge over the railway line, ignoring all other roads joining from left and right. Just beyond this bridge the road forks: take the left-hand fork and enter Bere Alston again via "The Square". Turn left in the main street, and continue past the Edgcumbe and along Station Road again back to the station.

You might be a bit pushed to catch the train from Bere Alston at 2.53 p.m., so it is better to take your time and aim for the next one at 5.38 p.m. May I repeat that you should always check these train times, as they are liable to change.

———————— WALK FIVE ————————

MILTON ABBOT – HORSEBRIDGE – SYDENHAM DAMEREL

Moderate. First part mainly on roads, second half chiefly on green lanes (which can be very muddy after rain). Involves a 450 foot climb from the Tamar valley back to the start. 6½ miles. OS 1:50 000 Map 201, OS 1:25 000 Maps 1339 and 1340.

Take the B3362 Tavistock–Launceston Road to Milton Abbot. Turn off beside the church and park by the roadside at the bottom of the churchyard as for Walk Two.

Walk down the hill from your parking place and pass a small new housing development in a cul-de-sac on your right. At the bottom of the hill the tarmac road ceases and you enter a muddy lane which is a public bridleway. Follow this lane for about a quarter of a mile until it ends at a gate into a field. Go through the gate and bear slightly left up the field: you can just make out the line of the bridleway by a slight depression in the ground. It brings you eventually to a hunting gate in the top left-hand corner of the field.

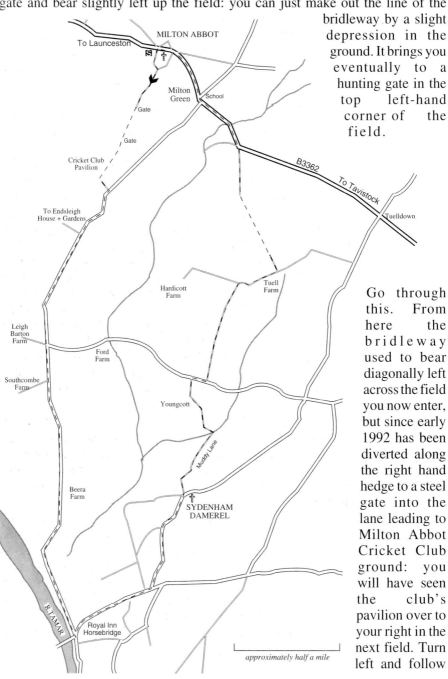

approximately half a mile

Go through this. From here the bridleway used to bear diagonally left across the field you now enter, but since early 1992 has been diverted along the right hand hedge to a steel gate into the lane leading to Milton Abbot Cricket Club ground: you will have seen the club's pavilion over to your right in the next field. Turn left and follow

18

this lane to its junction with the Milton Abbot–Horsebridge road.

Turn right along the road and follow it past the entrances to the Endsleigh Nurseries and to the house and gardens on your right. Continue along this road, which is fairly quiet but by no means devoid of traffic, for two miles as it descends into the Tamar valley and then follows the river for a short distance to Horsebridge, with its pub and ancient (1437) bridge crossing over into Cornwall. The name "Horsebridge" is said to derive from the Saxon leader Horsa, who had a bit of a dingdong with Celtic tribesmen on Hingston Down nearby.

The pub is called the Royal Inn, and has an interesting history: centuries ago it was called "The Packhorse", but was renamed "The Royal" in honour of Charles I. Considering how long this establishment has been dispensing booze it is odd to think that it began life as a convent. It also has the rare distinction of brewing its own beer, and very good it is, too. They do three different strengths (1038, 1045, and 1060 OG). They also sell various other real ales and do excellent meals and snacks. They are understandably particular here about muddy boots and wellies – if you are wearing them you have to go into the slate-floored public bar.

After lunch, turn right as you leave the pub and start climbing the hill signposted Sydenham Damerel. In half a mile, take a similarly signposted turning on your left, which brings you into this pleasant little hamlet in another half mile. Just past the church and the old village school (now converted into a dwelling), the road swings around to the right: do not follow it, but continue walking in the same northerly direction you have been following down a track on the left leading slightly downhill past a house and garage. This is a green lane leading down into a shallow valley, and can be extremely muddy at the bottom: I nearly lost my wellies here once. Note the field gate on the right here: it is much more interesting than the normal boring modern steel gate, having been made by an imaginative welder out of various bits of old farm machinery. Worse things are shown at the Tate Gallery!

The lane then climbs out of the valley, up what is often a virtual stream bed in wet weather, past some rather ruinous farm buildings at Youngcott. It then emerges on to a road. Turn right, and in 25 yards or so you will see another green lane turning off on your left. Take this, and continue climbing. This lane is also muddy and uneven, but not as bad as the last one. It passes a wood of tall beeches, emerging on to another road in half a mile.

Turn right and continue for about a quarter of a mile to Tuell farm. Turn left up the lane (signposted Public Bridleway) opposite the farmhouse, go between the farm buildings and through the gate. Follow the right-hand hedge uphill to the top of the field, ignoring the gateway on your right about two thirds of the way up. Go through the gate at the top of the field and cross the next field diagonally to a gateway you will see in the bottom left-hand corner. This leads into a lane which descends to the main road in the little valley just before you get to Milton Green. Walk cautiously here until you get to Milton Green, for there are no pavements until you reach there and the road is busy, and fairly narrow and winding at this point.

OLDMILL – LUCKETT – HORSEBRIDGE

Fairly easy, except for the 500-foot climb on the return trip! The walk is along quiet lanes and includes tracks and footpaths which can be muddy in wet weather. 6½ miles. OS 1:50 000 Map 201, OS 1:25 000 Map 1339.

This is a walk on the opposite (Cornish) side of the Tamar valley to the previous walk, and also uses the Royal Inn at Horsebridge for a lunch stop.

The walk starts from a car park at the base of Kit Hill. To get there, drive to Callington, then from the traffic lights in the centre of the town take the A390 road towards Gunnislake and Tavistock. In one and a half miles you come to a lay-by (part of the old road) from which a road turns off left around the eastern flank of Kit Hill. Take this road.

If you have the time, it is worth making a diversion to the top of Kit Hill: you will see the track on your left in another half a mile. The whole of Kit Hill is covered with evidence of mining activity ancient and fairly modern, and there are also many signs of prehistoric human occupation. From the summit (1100 feet) there are marvellous views in all directions over the Devon–Cornwall border country. A common adage all over the area is that if you can see Kit Hill clearly, it's going to rain, and if you can't see it, it **is** raining.

About a quarter of a mile beyond the bottom of the Kit Hill track you come to a crossroads (Monkscross). Turn left here on to the B3257, and in three-quarters of a mile, just opposite the turning to Downgate, a rather inconspicuous wooden sign indicates a car park on your left at the base of Kit Hill. Park here: it is actually a part of the old railway line from Kelly Bray and Callington – an inclined plane from the quarries higher up terminated here.

Cross the road from this car park and go down the road opposite towards Downgate. In about a third of a mile, opposite a road joining from the left, you will see a lane turning off on the right beside a house. This is a public footpath, although at the time of writing there is no sign to confirm it. Go down this: the concrete surface at the start soon gives way to mud much churned up by horses, but the edges aren't too bad. This track brings you out on to a road in a quarter of a mile. On the opposite side of the road is another track: carry on down this and you come out in the tiny hamlet of Oldmill.

Turn right along the road at the bottom of the track, then almost immediately right again on to a short grassy track between a stream and a house. Climb the stile beside the gate here, and you find yourself following a very pleasant woodland track along the valley bottom. A short distance along this you will see a mine dump on your right, part of an old copper mine called Wheal Sheba.

The track eventually emerges via another stile on to a road near New Mill Cottage. This road fords the stream here, but you can cross dry-shod via a small footbridge. Turn left up the short, fairly steep hill to Broadgate crossroads and turn right for Luckett here. As you approach this small village you can see over to your right on the other side of the valley the dumps, chimney, and ruined buildings of the old Wheal Martha, later known as New Great Consols. This was

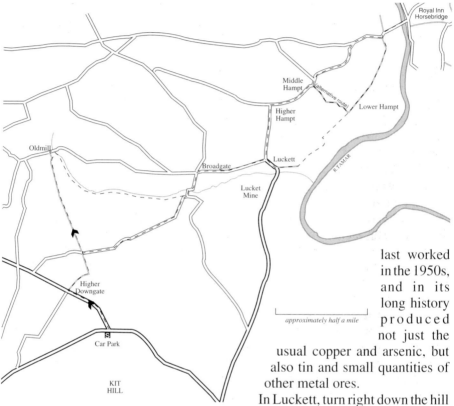

approximately half a mile

last worked in the 1950s, and in its long history produced not just the usual copper and arsenic, but also tin and small quantities of other metal ores.

In Luckett, turn right down the hill through the village, then at the bottom turn left just before the bridge in front of a row of cottages. Carry on to the end of this track and go through the gate into a wide meadow alongside the banks of the Tamar. This is a public footpath, but again at the time of writing there are no signs to confirm it. Follow the left-hand hedge right along to where it bears off to the left, and continue following it until it brings you to a gate in the left-hand corner of the field. Go through this gate – you will see in front of you to the right a couple of stone slabs spanning a small stream which runs down across the fields to the Tamar. Cross these and follow the track: in a few yards you come to a couple of lengths of telegraph pole barring a gap into the next field. Climb these and continue along by the right-hand hedge until you come to a gateway beside a corrugated iron shed. This leads you into the lane down to Lower Hampt Farm.

Turn right to follow this lane along beside the farm, carrying straight on past Wadlands Transport workshops (don't turn right down into the farmyard). Beyond the workshops a stretch of rough tarmac leads between several derelict cars and lorries into a delightful grassy lane which will bring you out on to the Stoke Climsland–Horsebridge road in half a mile. Turn right, cross the bridge over the Tamar into Devon, turn left on the other side of the bridge and you come to the Royal Inn in a few yards. There are some pictures in the lounge bar of the flooding which occurred here in torrential rain some years ago.

After lunch, retrace your steps back over the ancient bridge. You can carry on up the hill and turn left in a couple of hundred yards, but I think it is pleasanter to go back along the grassy lane past Lower Hampt Farm, and instead of going back across the fields, carry on up the lane to where it joins the road at Middle Hampt. Turn left along the road (or carry straight on if you decided to take the road route), and in a quarter of a mile turn left for Luckett by the restored chapel at Higher Hampt. A little way down this road you will see an old stone trough in the hedge with a rough stone gutter leading into it from the field behind.

Turn right in Luckett along the road you followed earlier. Along here you pass another old trough and stone gutter on your right, but unlike the one at Higher Hampt this one usually has water running through it. When you reach the crossroads at Broadgate, turn left down to the ford again. You now have a choice: from here you can either go back the way you came, through the woods and up the track, or take the right-hand road from the ford up towards Downgate. The latter is the shorter route, but whichever way you choose you still have to climb 500 feet! If you take the road, in three-quarters of a mile you come to the point where the track you followed down to Oldmill crosses it: take the left-hand track and you come out on the road at Higher Downgate. Turn left to return to the car park.

WALK SEVEN

WEST DOWN – DOUBLE WATERS – BUCKLAND MONACHORUM

Fairly easy, but some quite stiff climbs. 5 miles. OS 1:50 000 Map 201, OS 1:25 000 Maps 1340 and 1349.

Turn off the A386 Plymouth–Tavistock road opposite the Halfway House at Grenofen. About three-quarters of a mile along this road, just past a radio mast, turn left at the crossroads. This will bring you to a moorgate in about half a mile. Park by the hedge just inside the gate.

Follow the track downhill into the valley, ignoring tracks turning off to the left. Eventually you enter woodland, and the track takes you around a bend to the right by a cottage. You then descend to the valley floor beside the River Walkham. Follow the path to the right behind a rocky outcrop and cross the river by a wooden footbridge. The Tavy joins the Walkham here, hence the name "Double Waters".

From the bridge, climb up to the track you will see in front of you, and follow it to the right. This is the site of Virtuous Lady Mine, which is said to have been first worked in the reign of Queen Elizabeth I, hence the name. You will see various mine dumps, the mine captain's house and an adit in the next few hundred yards.

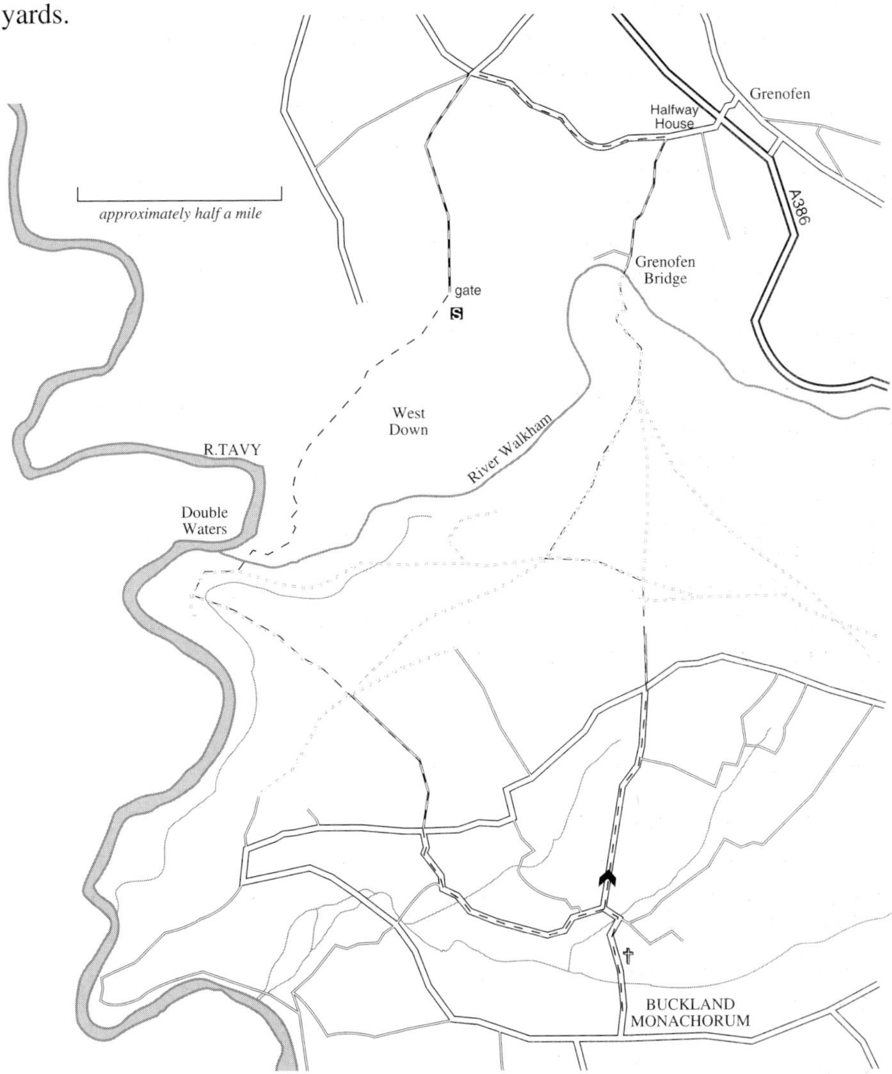

approximately half a mile

Grenofen

Halfway House

Grenofen Bridge

A386

gate

West Down

River Walkham

R.TAVY

Double Waters

BUCKLAND MONACHORUM

The track now climbs fairly steeply out of the Tavy valley and across the down to a moorgate which leads into a lane to Coppicetown crossroads. Carry straight on here and follow the lane into the village of Buckland Monachorum. If you want to know how to pronounce the second word of this name, this piece of doggerel might give you a clue, perhaps:

If you want to stagger 'em — Say Monaggerem,
To preserve decorum — Say MonaCHORum.

Anyway, it means Buckland of the Monks, as they inhabited nearby Buckland Abbey until the Dissolution of the Monasteries. Thereafter it became a desirable residence for the local big shots, notably Sir Francis Drake, who lived there when he wasn't sailing round the world, looting Spanish treasure, defeating the Spanish Armada, building leats and being MP for Plymouth: he lived a full life. The village also has a splendid pub, the Drake Manor, where you may obtain excellent food and drink.

After lunch, retrace your steps through the village. Don't turn right by the little roundabout where the bus turns round, but carry on and take the next right. This road climbs steadily to a crossroads. Carry straight on up the hill here until you reach a gate on to the open downland. Follow the track down the hill for about 200 yards, then turn off right along a rough grassy track much used by horses. Where the track divides, bear off to the left down into the valley through Sticklepath Wood. This track is very steep and rocky, but brings you eventually down to Grenofen Bridge over the Walkham. There are numerous mining remains in this area. Cross the bridge and climb the fairly steep hill to the road you drove along earlier. Turn left, follow this to the crossroads just beyond the radio mast, then turn left again to return to your car.

If you want to shorten this walk slightly, don't turn right along the grassy ride but continue on down the track from the moorgate, which will bring you back to Double Waters in one mile.

WALK EIGHT

TAVISTOCK CANAL – CREASE LANE

Easy. The first part, along the canal towpath, is level but can be muddy. This is followed by a climb up the old Gunnislake–Tavistock road, after which the route follows quiet lanes. I am told that the only convenient pub on this walk closed down recently, so it is advisable to take a packed lunch. 5 miles. OS 1:50 000 Map 201, OS 1:25 000 Map 1340.

Just as you enter Tavistock and before you cross West Bridge over the Tavy, a road called Pixon Lane turns off to the right. Follow it along beside the park known as The Meadows – just after it swings around to the right and starts to go uphill you will find two car parks: in the first one on the left you have to pay, but the one a little further up the hill on the right is free.

Go back down the hill after parking and enter The Meadows. Cross to the canal towpath on the far side and follow it to the main Plymouth road. Go over the pelican crossing and pick up the towpath on the other side of the road by descending some steps. A board here gives information about items of interest in the immediate vicinity, such as Fitzford gatehouse and cottages which you will see on your right. The latter were built for workers at the numerous mines in the area by the seventh Duke of Bedford with some of his considerable mining royalties. The district abounds in groups of cottages of this type.

Tavistock canal was constructed by John Taylor, the manager at Wheal

Friendship mine at Mary Tavy, in the early years of the nineteenth century. It took no less than fourteen years to build, mainly because of the difficulty of constructing a one and a half-mile tunnel through unexpectedly hard rock under Morwell Down; it was finally opened in 1817. Its purpose was the transport of

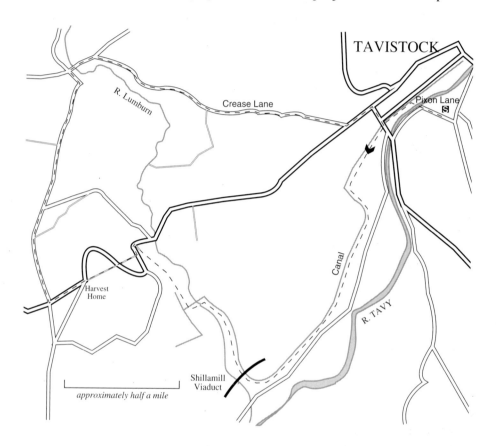

approximately half a mile

Wheal Friendship's copper, Dartmoor granite and slate from Mill Hill quarries to the river port of Morwellham for shipment, and carrying coal, limestone and manure in the other direction. As the port is some 240 feet below the end of the canal, goods from the barges were loaded on to wagons and lowered down an inclined plane. The energy of the canal water plunging down into the Tamar is put to good use today in a hydroelectric generating plant feeding power into the national grid.

The canal runs along beside Tavistock Comprehensive School grounds at first, but soon leaves these behind, in about a mile flowing past Crowndale Farm. An information board here tells you about the canal and also about Sir Francis Drake, who is reputed to have been born in a long-vanished house in this area. That's why a statue of him, the original of the one on Plymouth Hoe, stands in the middle of

25

the roundabout near the road bridge over the canal in Tavistock. At Crowndale the canal, and the old Southern Region main line you can see at the top of the field on the right, pass through the site of an old copper mine, but the area's main claim to fame nowadays is as the site of Tavistock's sewage works and refuse tip. What a come-down.

The canal now starts to curve around the hillside away from the Tavy valley into the tributary valley of the Lumburn, passing under the impressive arches of Shillamill viaduct as it does so. This viaduct may possibly carry trains again if the line is reopened from Bere Alston to Tavistock.

About half a mile further on the canal makes a 90 degree turn to the left on to an embankment and aqueduct which carries it over the Lumburn. Unfortunately it is not possible to follow the towpath as far as the mouth of the tunnel: a South West Electricity Board notice informs you that it is private property beyond that point. However, the footpath crosses the canal by a concrete bridge and runs along beside a dry ditch. This is all that remains of the Mill Hill Cut, a branch of the canal which used to carry slate from Mill Hill Quarries about one and a quarter miles to the north. Follow the path until it reaches the Tavistock–Gunnislake road at Lumburn. Turn left, and in a very few yards you will see a rough lane leading steeply uphill on your right. This is the old road – although it is much steeper than the modern road's zig-zag ascent it is much pleasanter walking. Follow it up the hill, crossing the modern road half-way up. Exercise great caution here: the old road emerges straight on to the new with very limited visibility – you could step straight out of the nineteenth century into the twentieth with potentially disastrous consequences. The next section of the old road will bring you out in the car park of the Harvest Home Inn, where you could have had lunch if it was open!

Turn left along the main Gunnislake road (not the minor road which turns left immediately beside the pub) and follow it for about 250 yards. Care is needed here, as it is a fast stretch of road and fairly busy. Take the first turning right, a quiet lane which climbs past the turnings to Colcharton and Newton. Opposite the latter turning is an interesting old granite milepost which says in bold letters "to THE QUAYS – 2 miles", i.e. to Morwellham. The lane then descends into the upper Lumburn valley and comes to a crossroads. The old Mill Hill Cut can be traced up the Lumburn valley in places, and approaching the crossroads you can see to your left the arch of the old bridge which carried the road to Chipshop over it. If you were to go straight on past the row of handsome quarrymen's cottages, you would come to Mill Hill quarry, the destination of the Mill Hill Cut. However, we will turn right here and cross Middle Lumburn Bridge, then right again in a couple of hundred yards. This road is Crease Lane, and climbs steadily up to Crease Farm before descending into Tavistock. There are splendid views across North Dartmoor from this stretch.

Crease Lane crosses the old Southern Region main line as it enters the outskirts of Tavistock, and joins the Gunnislake road near Fitzford Catholic church. Turn right at the bottom of the hill, pass Drake's statue, cross the road into the Meadows, which you then cross to return to your car.

Wheal Friendship & Hillbridge Leats

Fairly easy, but there are two problems with the first part of this walk: firstly, it is across open moorland, so is best avoided in misty or wintry conditions, and secondly it runs through the Army's Willsworthy live firing range, so you can't do it if firing is taking place, which is frequently. Times and areas of live firing are published in the *Western Morning News* on Fridays and are usually announced on BBC Radio Devon on 855 kHz between 7.35 and 7.40 and 8.35 and 8.40 a.m. If you miss these, ring Plymouth 701924 for a recorded message giving the current week's information. If all else fails look for the red flags which are flown on prominent hilltops in the vicinity when firing is in progress. Firing does not take place during August. Also, I would think that this walk would be unsuitable for large dogs because of the difficulty of getting them up the vertical iron steps at Hill Bridge. 5½ miles. OS 1:50 000 Map 201, OS 1:25 000 Maps 1327 (SX48/58) and 1340.

From Tavistock take the A386 Okehampton road to Mary Tavy, and just before you enter the village turn right by the Mary Tavy Inn. In about a quarter of a mile you come to a T-junction: turn left here, and then right in another quarter of a mile. Follow this road for two miles through the hamlet of Horndon to where the road makes a sharp right-hand bend. Just after this you come to a junction: bear left here, then left again at the next junction by Will Farm and riding stables, and follow the road through Willsworthy to where it finishes at Lanehead. Park in the car park here, and check to see that no red flags are flying on White Hill or Ger Tor to the north, or at Lanehead itself.

Head north from the Lanehead car park slightly uphill across the open moor, making for the leat embankment you will see about a quarter of a mile ahead of you. Turn left along the leatside path, following it downstream. This is the Wheal Friendship or Reddaford leat, which abstracts its water from the Tavy at a weir about a mile upstream in spectacular Tavy Cleave. Like the Tavistock Canal, it was engineered by John Taylor – its purpose was to take sufficient water to Wheal Friendship copper mine at Mary Tavy to drive its many water wheels for pumping, operating stamps and so forth.

The leat soon reaches an aqueduct over the Willsworthy Brook, where it swings sharply to the south-east and starts to run alongside the Willsworthy range. Several footbridges and one bridge for wheeled traffic cross the leat on this stretch, it is also crossed by the Lych Way along which corpses used to be carried for burial at Lydford from the heart of the moor. This must have been an impossible journey in winter, and there is probably a grain of truth in the old Dartmoor joke about the benighted traveller being given shelter in an isolated farmhouse one stormy night who opened a chest in his room to find the body of an old man in it. He rushed downstairs and blurted out his discovery to the farmer, who calmly replied, "Aw, 'tis only granfer – us lted 'un down for the winter!"

Another waterway now approaches Wheal Friendship leat running parallel with it a few yards away. This is Wheal Jewell leat, yet another of John Taylor's works, which abstracts its water from the Walla Brook behind White Hill and supplied the water wheels of the mine of the same name. The site of this mine is now occupied by the long, narrow Wheal Jewell reservoir you are approaching, which supplies a hydroelectric generating plant at Mary Tavy.

It is not possible to continue along the leat to this reservoir, as it is pretty firmly fenced off, so when you reach this fence branch off left to a gate you will see below you, then follow the posts to the head of a very rough, muddy lane, much chewed up by horses' hooves, which will bring you out on to the road you drove along to Lanehead earlier, just on the sharp bend near Will Farm. Turn right along the road – you will reach Horndon in one mile. Just out on the Mary Tavy side of this small village there is a splendid pub called "The Elephant's Nest" (formerly the New Inn), where good food

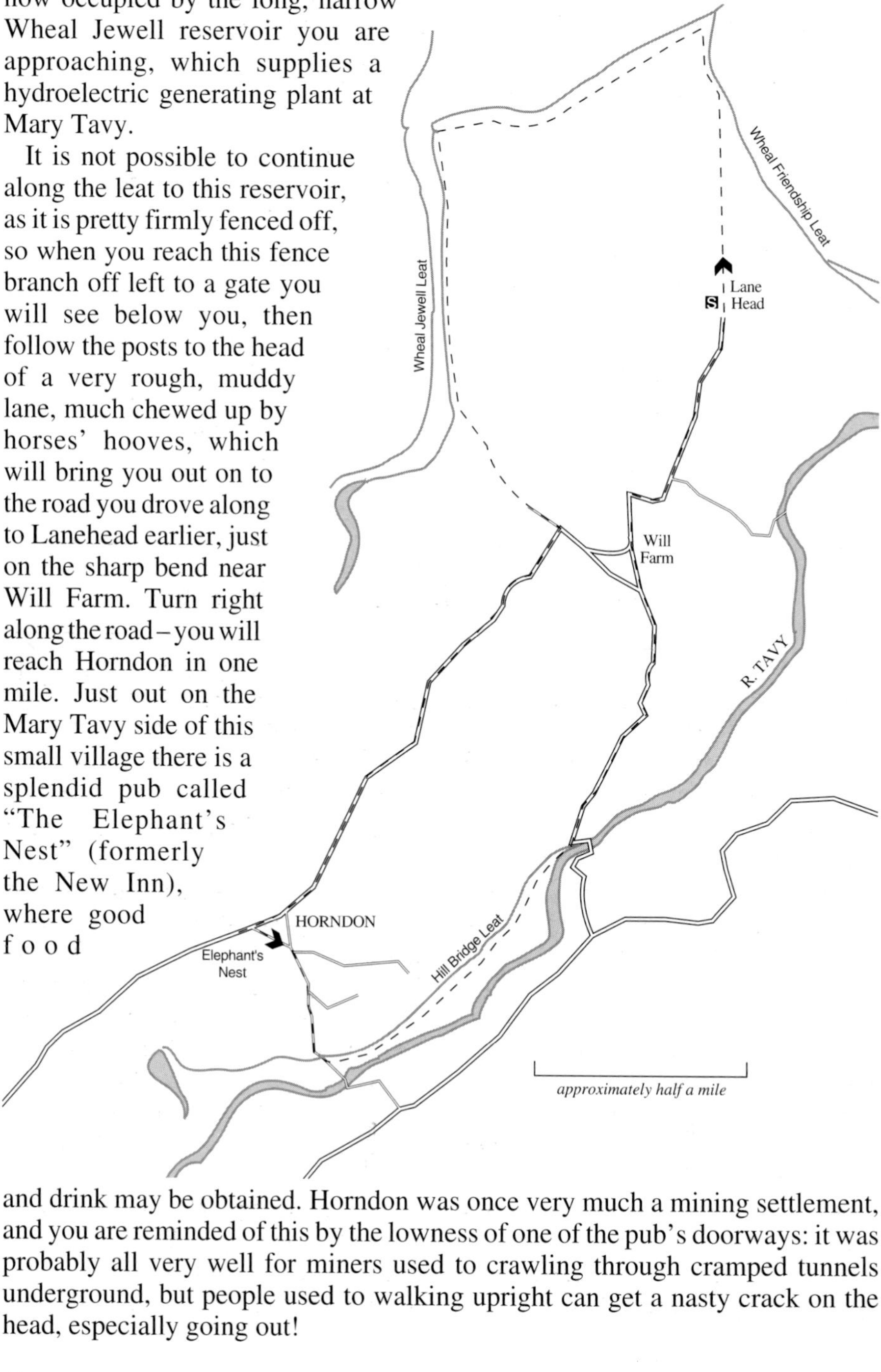

Wheal Friendship Leat

Wheal Jewell Leat

Lane Head

Will Farm

R. TAVY

HORNDON

Elephant's Nest

Hill Bridge Leat

approximately half a mile

and drink may be obtained. Horndon was once very much a mining settlement, and you are reminded of this by the lowness of one of the pub's doorways: it was probably all very well for miners used to crawling through cramped tunnels underground, but people used to walking upright can get a nasty crack on the head, especially going out!

After lunch, retrace your steps back into Horndon then turn right by the telephone box. This brings you into a rough lane leading downhill towards the Tavy valley (Horndon Lane). Before it reaches the river, however, it crosses the Hill Bridge Leat. This is another leat constructed to supply Wheal Friendship, and like the one we walked along earlier now supplies the hydroelectric plant at Mary Tavy.

Go through the gate on the left then walk along the right bank of the leat upstream (a South West Electricity Board notice forbids entry downstream). This is a very picturesque stretch of leat running above the Tavy with the bulk of Cudlipptown Down on the other side of the valley. It becomes increasingly rocky as you proceed – at one point you pass a huge outcrop, known appropriately as Big Rock, on the other bank. After this the leat enters a delightful wooded area (Creason Wood) before it reaches its head weir at Hill Bridge. Here you cross it to gain entry to the road via a set of iron dog-steps set in the wall. Whatever they may be called, they are not suitable for dogs, and you would have a problem getting a dog of any size up here. Turn left up the hill, bear right at the fork near Will Farm, then continue through Willsworthy to Lanehead and your car.

Walk Ten
Milton Abbot – Bradstone – Kelly

Moderate. Includes one bridleway, which can be very muddy, two footpaths, several quiet lanes, and involves a climb of 540 feet from the banks of the Tamar to the highest point of the walk. There is no pub on the walk, so you will need to take a packed lunch. 6½ miles. OS 1:50 000 Map 201, OS 1:25 000 Maps 1326 and 1340.

Like Walks Two and Five, this one starts from Milton Abbot on the B3362 Tavistock–Launceston road, so turn off by the church as before and park by the roadside below the churchyard.

We start by doing the last part of Walk Two in reverse. Cross the main road and go up the lane opposite the church. At the top of this is a Public Footpath sign indicating a stile into a long narrow field. Go up this field to a gap at the top left-hand corner into the top corner of another field, where you immediately turn right through a gateway into another field. Cross this one diagonally to the left to a triple stile over two lots of sheep wire and a hedge. Cross the next field diagonally to the left to a stile in the left-hand corner, then in the next field follow the left-hand hedge across two fields until you come to a stile into the road. There are often sheep in these fields, so keep dogs under close control. Large dogs might find many of these stiles difficult.

Turn left along the road: along this stretch is the highest point of the walk (680 feet). As you might expect there are magnificent views up the Tamar valley to Launceston, and over towards Bodmin Moor in the west, looming over the Lynher valley. In one and a half miles another road joins from the left: here there is an old milestone at the meeting of the ways. Just after this you come to the oddly-named hamlet of Felldownhead, which has a home-made roadsign as you enter which says, "Slow! Children and other Animals". You pass livery stables, then by the turning to Bradstone and Kelly stands Felldownhead Farm, where farm cider has been made for generations. It is now marketed under the name Countryman Farm Cider – if you call in there they will give you a taste of their various brews (dry, medium dry, and medium sweet) so that you can decide which you prefer before buying; they will also show you around and explain the process if you wish. In October you can see the cider actually being made. I can assure you it is excellent stuff, 6.5% alcohol – I wonder if that's how the place got its name?

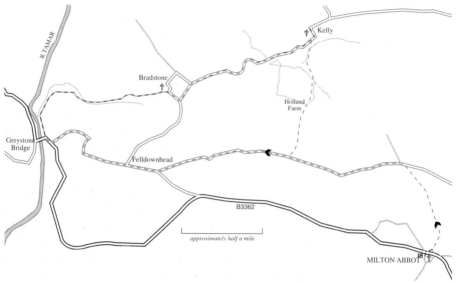

Walk on down the hill past the entrance to Pallastreet Farm, with a good view of the extensive quarry workings just across the Tamar in Cornwall. You pass another old granite milestone on the first bend, but passing traffic makes it no place to linger and decipher it. At the bottom there is a drinking fountain which bears the legend:

    1894
    RK
    DRINK
    AND BE
    THANKFUL

Turn right to walk along the main road for a few yards towards Greystone Bridge crossing the Tamar into Cornwall: this is so narrow that traffic is restricted to single file, controlled by traffic lights. Just before reaching the bridge, take the unsurfaced lane leading off to the right. At the time of writing there is no Public Bridleway sign here, although there is one at the other end.

The lane follows the Tamar for about a quarter of a mile before swinging away and starting to climb up a tributary valley. You pass a farm and go past a number of farm buildings, where the track gets pretty muddy because of the passage of tractors. By the last shed bear right through a gate and continue to climb for a short distance before the track drops to a ford across the stream. Go through another gate, after which the track runs through woodland and is fairly level for a while, but very squishy. On your right you will see the back of Pallastreet farm, and a mini-assault course of old tyres, climbing nets and ladders among the bushes by the stream.

The track then starts to climb steadily, and shortly brings you to Coombemills, where you may see a number of deer behind the electric fence. A little further on you emerge on to the road at Bradstone near the church, which is dedicated to St. Nonna, a female Welsh saint. Bradstone is a tiny hamlet and, apart from the church, its most striking feature is the impressive gatehouse to Bradstone manor, which you will see to your left past the church. I am told that this used to be the dwelling of the family coachman.

After inspecting the gatehouse, retrace your steps past the end of the bridleway and continue to a T-junction. Turn left, then follow this fairly quiet road for a mile to Kelly, which soon comes into view, prompting a friend of mine to remark at this point that there seemed to be more churches than houses in this area. Just before you enter the hamlet of Kelly you will notice a footpath sign and stile on your right. This is the one you want, but first it is well worth going on a few yards to have a look at Kelly.

Kelly House is a handsome Georgian building, home of the Kelly family for many generations. In terms of the family history, though, it is comparatively modern, for there were Kellys here for centuries before it was built. The church (dedicated to St. Mary) has many family memorials. By the entrance to the stable yard, with its elegant but sadly dilapidated mews and coachhouses, stands a curious tall, narrow building raised off the ground on brick piers. This was a granary, and the purpose of raising it above ground level was to deny access to rats. There is a Victorian post box set in one wall.

Retrace your steps to the footpath sign and climb the stile. Go straight down the field and across a little bridge over the stream you will see straight in front of you. Turn right, then follow the left bank of the stream until you see a stile in the hedge on your left. Climb this, then head slightly to your right across the field, gradually heading down towards another stream until you see a stile and a couple of footbridges. Cross these, and another stile on the other side, and climb steeply up the field, bearing slightly left. You will shortly see Holland Farm in front of you. Go through the gate into the busy yard of this dairy farm and through the gate on the other side. Pass in front of the farmhouse and go up the concrete road which climbs the hill. This will bring you out on to the road you walked along on the way out. Turn left – in just under a mile you come to the footpath sign and stile at the start of the footpath leading back to Milton Abbot.

OTHER "WALKS" BOOKS

WALKS IN THE SHADOW OF DARTMOOR, *Denis McCallum*

Another book from the pen (and feet!) of the author of this book. This time Denis explores the countryside beneath Dartmoor's hills – places off the beaten track which are well worth a pedestrian visit.

WALKS IN THE SOUTH HAMS, *Brian Carter*

Written in his own unique style, Brian Carter, presenter of the highly acclaimed "Dartmoor – the Threatened Wilderness", describes some wonderful strolls from around the beautiful South Hams.

WALKING 'With a Tired Terrier' IN AND AROUND TORBAY, *Brian Carter*

Forget the image you may have of Torbay for, like Plymouth, it doesn't take long to find great walking country. Brian Carter is at his very best in this entertaining book.

RAMBLING IN THE PLYMOUTH COUNTRYSIDE, *Woolley & Lister*

Plymouth is blessed with having some extremely beautiful countryside as its back garden. This books contains a variety of walks on all sides of the city.

TEN FAMILY WALKS ON DARTMOOR, *Sally and Chips Barber*

This is the ideal guide for people who want a gentle baptism to Dartmoor walking. It contains ten walks up to about six miles long and is packed with entertaining facts about the places visited.

TEN FAMILY WALKS IN EAST DEVON, *Sally and Chips Barber*

Written and presented in an identical format, this book explores the driest part of Devon. Ten glorious little walks of up to 5 miles long to savour all that is best in 'sunny' East Devon.

THE TEMPLER WAY, *Derek Beavis*

As the title suggests, this is a guide to the walk that starts at Haytor and finishes at Teignmouth. It is an invaluable guide to an extremely pleasant jaunt through a variety of landscapes.

THE GREAT WALKS OF DARTMOOR, *Terry Bound*

Terry Bound, member of the Long Distance Walking Association, has compiled in this brilliant book all the major walks – Ten Tors, Abbots Way, North-South, OATS walk and many more.

DIARY OF A DARTMOOR WALKER, *Chips Barber*

This is the one book that most Dartmoor enthusiasts will treasure as, written in an amusing and entertaining way, it presents a real picture of Dartmoor, reflecting the trials and tribulations of any avid Dartmoor walker.

DIARY OF A DEVONSHIRE WALKER, *Chips Barber*

This is the sequel to the above mentioned book and includes many more misadventures like the joys of leading an incontinence clinic on a moorland ramble or tripping over courting couples whilst out on evening excursions ... you get the picture? Get the book!